# Dear Baby,
## Get Out!

*Angela Grout*

# Dear Baby, Get Out!

*A Hysterical & Neurotic Story of the
Last Days of Pregnancy*

## By
## Angela Grout

Copyright © 2016 Angela Grout
Editor: Patricia Fry

Cover: iStock

Unless otherwise indicated, all writings are by the author.

For Information Contact:
Angela Grout
430 Main St
Agawam, MA 01001
413-786-7427

Printed in the USA

*Dear Baby, Get Out!*

*A Hysterical & Neurotic Story of the
Last Days of Pregnancy*

*Angela Grout*

Also written by Angela Grout

*An Angel's Journey*

# The Natural Order of Contents

*Angela Grout*

*For*

*Maggie & Molly*

*Thank you for allowing me to be part of your journey and for allowing me to share part of mine…YOU!*

*Angela Grout*

# *1*

# *To Do*

I am waiting to give birth and nothing is happening. This is as exciting as watching paint dry. I'm bored and frustrated. I have been trying to keep as busy as possible. I've washed all the sheets on all four beds in the house, cleaned the bathrooms, dusted the furniture, swept the porch, and even used Lysol wipes to clean the  siding on the porch!

The baby's room is completely set up. Not only are the furniture and decorations in place, but all the baby clothes have been washed, folded, and put away in drawers labeling the contents. Yes, I labeled the drawers in case I get a bout of amnesia during delivery and forget where I put everything.

The changing table in the baby's room as well as the mini-changing station I created in the downstairs living room only need a baby now. All the medicines are prepared to be used in case of emergency. I have removed all the plastic packaging so, while holding a fussy baby, I won't have to waste any time trying to peel off that darn wrapping.

Every diaper package, every box of wipes, and even the diaper crème tubes are prepped and ready for action. It just made sense to make sure I can grab anything with one hand at any given moment.

The rocking chair is ready. I have stocked the table to the right with a bottle of water, a stack of burp cloths, a glow-in-the-dark clock, a journal with a pen to record all the feedings, and I have even assembled a basket of books to read. Of course the books are in alphabetical order with a few adjustments to sizing so they would fit in the eight-by-twelve inch rectangular pink gingham lined basket that I received as a shower gift.

As I glance at that table, I check to make sure the twenty-five watt bulb I installed works with the pull chain; it does. Maybe I should put a spare light bulb near it, just in case it burns out during a midnight feeding.

I notice the cordless phone, and quickly check to see if it is on silent. It is. The monitor is running with the cordless monitor in my bedroom at the moment and the stationary monitor in the kitchen. The kitchen monitor is plugged in, but not turned on. I tested it yesterday when my six-year-old stood in the crib and put on a show while I watched from the kitchen. It works.

Hmmm...What else needs to be done?

The extra changing pads are within arm's reach, along with a stack of new sheets, just in case there's an explosion in the crib in the middle of the night. The mobile is ready for use and I've taken all the stuffed animals and pillows out of the crib so she won't roll onto them and suffocate. The bumper is secure around the crib. I had heard a rumor that they want to ban bumpers so babies can't suffocate in them. But without them, their little legs could get stuck in the bars. I'm proud of the mesh bumper I found. It is breathable and protects the slots of the crib from wandering little feet.

The bassinet is set up in the master bedroom next to my side of the bed along with additional burp cloths, and a pacifier. I installed a wedge so the baby can lie on her side and not roll into the side of the bassinette and suffocate. My girlfriends say it will work. I readjust the two triangular pillows of the wedge. Because I don't know how wide the baby is yet, I had to guess and I linked the first set of three Velcro straps together. Thank goodness the hard side of the Velcro is on the bottom because it could scratch the baby's skin. I make a mental note to keep an eye on that.

I find myself wandering through the house looking for something to do. Nothing.

I have pre-addressed all the envelopes for her birth announcement. I cannot stuff them with the photo yet as this baby has yet to debut for a photo! Not only do I not know what she looks like, but I don't have any stats on her. She doesn't even have a name! I suppose I could spend some time considering names, but I'm too exhausted for that right now. I secretly hope she comes out with a name tag. I've spent many nights doodling, reading name books, and discussing names with my husband, but nothing has stuck yet.

Let's see, my iPod is updated, my work folders are organized, I have shopped until I can't find anything else to buy; seriously!

The car has been Jiffy Lubed and washed. I've made an appointment for new brakes for tomorrow. If I'm in labor tomorrow, my father-in-law will take the car in, so that backup plan is ready.

The refrigerator and pantry are stocked. The grocery list is hanging blank on the outside of the pantry door. I almost wrote Cheerios, but remembered I have two boxes in the basement and, by the time the baby is eating them, I probably can get to a store to buy more. I hope.

Opening the freezer, I note that ten of the fifteen meals I have prepared are neatly lined up so I can see the labels I put on them. Meat Lasagna, Vegetable Lasagna, Chicken Crescent Squares, Baked Ziti, Chicken and Rice Casserole, Meatballs, Broccoli Chicken Casserole, Chili, Chicken Soup, Sausage with Peppers, and Stuffed Shells. Each label has the date and cooking information on them. The other five meals are in the basement refrigerator with some Omaha steaks and twice-baked potatoes for another easy planned meal.

I have cleaned out one cabinet in the kitchen above the counter that holds the mail basket for baby items. The bottles and nipples are stacked neatly. I hope the baby can use these kinds, if not, thank God,

Amazon has one-day shipping. I reach into a drawer and take out a pen. I place the pen in the baby's cabinet next to the breast pump labels. The labels are in a neat pile but, after looking at them and realizing that a gust of wind could scatter them, I quickly put them into a small Tupperware container. I count three boxes of breast milk storage bags. There are thirty in each, so I hope that will be enough. Again, good thing Amazon will ship in one day.

All the baby essentials are ready. The high chair is assembled and there are bibs ready for use. I know I'll have to rewash them since they'll probably get dusty draped over the chair for the months that will pass before she can actually wear them. I may have to get more batteries from the basement soon for the swing as my six-year-old has been using in daily for her Bitty Baby.

The Exersaucer and the Giggle Garden Activity Gym are lined up next to the couch, along with a basket of toys, rattles, and stuffed animals that are safe for infants. My husband installed all the child gates in the stairwells, both up and downstairs, as well as around the fireplace. I also made him add bumpers to the corners of all the tables and insert outlet protectors all over the house. I wanted to switch out all our blinds so the baby wouldn't play with the cord and get hurt. Instead, I cut the cords and installed curtain holders up high to wrap them around.

The car seats are installed in both cars, along with giant mirrors, sunshades, and a basket of DVDs. The DVDs at this point are mainly for the six-year-old, but I did stock a Baby Einstein in there at least for musical purposes. Most of the Baby Einstein DVDs are in my bedroom where I assume she will be watching them when I shower.

I don't know what else I can do to prepare. If only I could start pumping milk, then I would feel more productive. My breasts are so huge that I probably could try. But since the milk doesn't come in until after she arrives, it's useless. Oh, my breasts are going to be killing me then! I did stock my bathroom with washcloths to wet with warm water if I have trouble with let-down, but I tried that last time and it only worked some of the time. It's difficult to breast feed when your breasts are like the Rock of Gibraltar.

Okay, so I can't pump milk yet, and I really don't know what else to do. The clock in the kitchen ticks loudly, reminding me of the extreme quietness. Tick Tick Tick…the calm before the storm. I'm trying to enjoy this peace and quiet, but it's actually boring. If only I would go into labor.

I have tried sex, spicy foods, bumpy car rides, long baths, bouncing on a birth ball, walking, and now I'm trying to relax. Ha-ha, me relax? I am trying.

Today is my due date. I truly assumed that I would have this baby before today. Three months ago I began labor and was put on bed rest. After the bed rest, things quieted down for about a month, then the contractions started again. Every night I was getting contractions three-to-four minutes apart for about twenty minutes then they just stopped.

Finally, three weeks ago, I lost my mucus plug. I figured this definitely was it. I went to the doctors, they said I was two centimeters and it could be any day, but they would rather me wait until my due date. Well that is today, so now what do I do? I realize that, in a week or even in a day, I won't have time to take a pee or blink ever again. However, today that's all I'm doing…peeing and blinking, and blinking and peeing. (Well, and trying to breath, walk, sit, and move comfortably.)

I have two theories at the moment; either this baby is really strong-willed or I'm not really pregnant—the doctors lied to me; I have a giant tumor and I'm going to die very soon.

Either way, I'm a sitting duck—sitting on my egg, or waiting to get shot out of the water. The doctor will induce labor in eight days if it doesn't happen before. They cannot evict this baby any earlier as the law says you have to be at least a week overdue.

I do hope this baby will leave without being forced. Maybe she is scared and I need to reassure her. I rub my belly and tell her about our beautiful home. Then I realize that, apparently, I have made her current home too comfortable. I tap my belly and say, "Come out and meet me." She kicks me back. Well she hears me.

Uh-oh, now she's really moving. She's so active in there; but I truly don't know how she has room to move because I can't breathe.

How am I going to convince her to get out? I was thinking I'd buy a pack of smokes and a bottle of Jim Beam and smoke her out…then it wouldn't be so comfortable inside and she would want out. She would really appreciate the fresh air and maybe I could catch my breath, too.

Maybe she is waiting for a big debut, but then she has seemed rather shy for the past ten months. In every ultrasound we've had, she always turned her head away so we couldn't see her face. She'd better get over this stage fright, as she will be in the spotlight very soon. It's a shame we couldn't see her face since the ultrasound images are so clear now. I think if I saw her features, then I would have a name for her at this point. Stubborn little girl.

Before I fall asleep each night, which I hope happens quickly now (as I'm as comfortable as I am going to get), I talk to her with my thoughts. Yes, I believe that she can hear my thoughts, which just goes to say how smart my daughter will be. She is constantly learning just by listening to my thoughts. I do hope she either tunes me out or doesn't understand when I'm fantasizing or cursing!

"Dear Baby, I love you. I pray that you are healthy and I will accept when you arrive as the perfect time. Please be safe in your journey here. Have pity on your poor mom as I am probably losing my mind, and it may get worse with two little girls in the house. Life is going to be fun. I'm sorry I don't have your name picked out yet. I wish you could give me a clue as to what it should be. Let's sleep well tonight. Maybe tomorrow you will come."

*Angela Grout*

# 2

# *Motivation*

Last night, she squirmed around for over an hour. It was actually pretty gross watching my skin stretch around like an alien was about to emerge. Not as gross as the night she turned completely around in my belly. That was over a month ago, but thinking about that night still makes me want to crawl out of my skin.

From the beginning, I thought she was breech. I often joked with my mother, saying that I thought a foot was hanging out of my vagina. I swear, if I didn't wear underwear, there would be no barrier between her and the world. She definitely would have pushed a foot out.

There were many days that I couldn't sit properly for fear I would break her ankle. Her kicks were so low that I still wonder if she was trying to walk out of the womb. That would be nice. Then I wouldn't have to push her out and endure labor.

Two months ago I arrived at the hospital with contractions less than two minutes apart for over two hours; they did an ultrasound and confirmed that she was breech. Doc said if she didn't turn on her own by thirty-six weeks, they would manually do it. I didn't ask what *manually* meant, but I had heard tales of having to get on all fours and have an arm or something stuck inside to move the baby to a head down position.

The nurse administered some steroid shots and gave me some anti-nausea medicine, which I desperately needed. The contractions made me feel as though I had motion sickness. Once I got some meds, the contractions stopped and they sent me home for bed rest.

Doc said no activity for one month. No stairs, no standing for long periods of time, and no exercise. Doc said I had to avoid going into labor for at least four weeks.

Those four weeks were long and quiet. My mom came over and washed everything in the house; she has an obsession with clean clothes. She folded all the baby's clothes and we stacked them neatly in the pre-labeled drawers I had created. She helped with all my husband's ironing and wouldn't allow me to even carry a glass of water while walking.

When the four weeks were over, I was sure I would go into labor. In fact, I was hoping, as I am now. I returned to work, stood for long periods, and walked a lot; but the only thing that developed was her hiccupping all the time. Apparently when a baby in the womb hiccups they are doing practice breaths. This baby was setting her goal to be a professional athlete in breathing.

One night, as I laid in bed as comfortable as possible, she began practicing breathing again, then all of a sudden my belly felt like it was going to burst open. I didn't know what was happening, but I laid on my back clutching the sheets with an obvious look of sheer terror. My husband noticed my vice grip on the sheets and asked, "Are you okay?"

He obviously could tell I wasn't, but I couldn't speak. I closed my eyes and held my breath as she proceeded to turn herself around inside me. Every bone took a turn of its own. Her leg bone, her elbow, her hip, a shoulder, another shoulder, even her butt seemed to take the turn. I looked down at my belly and wanted to puke. Straight branches seemed to be sliding around inside me, trying to poke through my skin.

After ten minutes, nothing emerged out and things settled down so my suffering was over for the moment. I could feel a foot kicking towards my heart and a hand moving whatever organ was in the way of her head resting gently in my pelvis.

I was so tired. I just wanted to fall asleep, but she had other intentions. Hiccups, then a kick, then another arm swoosh. She was really trying to get comfortable but her discomfort certainly kept me awake. Finally at two am, things quieted down; thanks to the dose of Benadryl I took for us. She then fell asleep and so did I.

I'm feeling motivated this morning. Perhaps it's an energy burst. The good news is my slippers fit today. My feet were so swollen yesterday that I actually stuck my feet in the snow a few times. But the slippers still didn't go on. It's exciting to be able to wear them today. My feet are bursting out of them, but they're on. It's pretty sad that my life has come down to the excitement of putting slippers on. In a few days, there will be much more to focus on.

I really wish I had a name for the baby, maybe if I called her name she would pop out. Ugh, that must be it. I just don't feel anything is right at the moment. Her sister wants Lexy, but I'm not feeling it. My husband told me to make a list, but I'm so exhausted. I just want it to be DONE. With my first pregnancy, I knew her name from the beginning, but with this little one, well she seems to not want to share. I feel guilty for not knowing what I want to call her? Well I did want to call her Lilliana, but everyone seems to be against that and, well, I'm just as stubborn as this baby and can't even think of another name.

It's like Rumpelstiltskin, I need to say her name and she will pop out. HELP. How hard does this have to be? I suppose since I'm so old that contributes to my lack of decision-making. For anyone thinking about waiting to have a baby, don't wait until you're thirty-eight. Thirty-eight is old for baby-making. The toll it takes on a mid-life body is crazy. Sore hips, loss of brain power, metabolism slow-down, extra weight, swollen parts, stuffy nose, and, well, I could go on and on. This baby and her placenta better weigh in at over forty pounds so that I can attempt the process of regaining my body back.

All right, enough negativity, I certainly don't want her to think I don't appreciate being selected as her spaceship to travel to earth. There are some plus sides to being pregnant, besides the obvious joy of the new baby to come. My breasts are huge and my husband does all the laundry, groceries, and transporting our other daughter to her activities. That's mainly because I have been on bed rest and have had strict instructions not to lift anything over five pounds. Which even if I wanted to, I don't know how I would, since my balance is off.

I've had more time to read, update photo albums, and respond to emails. Reading the emails sent by my family members does help the clock tick faster. However they mostly contain the same questions, "Did you have the baby yet?" Nope.

On another plus side, I don't feel a bit guilty for the eight sugar cookies I ate yesterday (yes I said eight), or the three sundaes I had last weekend. If you are what you eat, then I'm really sweet. And we know what little girls are made of; therefore there is no doubt that this is a girl.

Believe it or not, my other daughter is getting even more anxious than I am. She can't wait to be a big sister, and I know she will be the best big sister ever. She talks to the baby every night and tells her to come out. But little sister isn't listening. We have all agreed that this baby should be grounded until she's at least five for not listening.

I need to take full advantage of this sleeping baby in my belly right now, so I'm off to walk, walk, walk, walk, shop, shop, shop, shop, and try to forget about the delivery that lies ahead. Perhaps when she wakes up she'll want to get out of this constant moving machine.

*Angela Grout*

# 3

# *Crumbs*

I woke up at 3:00 am with contractions for over an hour. I really thought this would be it. I tried to walk around the house, but with each step, I stopped in pain and grabbed the molding around the door jam. After the third contraction, I banged on the wall hoping to alert my husband. I gradually banged my fist louder and louder as I couldn't speak, but he wasn't waking up.

When the contraction ended, I gently shook him in bed to inform him that I needed his help to time these things. As I shook him awake, he jumped up, freaked out that someone was about to hurt him. The thought crossed my mind because, when he jumped, I contracted again and couldn't tell him what was going on. He just looked at me and kept saying, "What do you want?"

Seriously, he can't tell I'm in pain? I pointed to my wrist as a signal to time the contraction, but he just said, "What do you want? Just tell me." How I wished we played charades more often, how can he not understand the wrist-pointing gesture? Idiot.

I waved him away, but just as quickly the contraction ended. "I was having a contraction," I said.

"How was I supposed to know that?" he asked.

"Really? I mean, really?" I could feel my belly clenching again. Getting mad wasn't going to stop these contractions, but I really was getting mad. Attempting to yell through the start of the next contraction, I tried to say, "I'm about to have a baby, and you have no idea why I'm waking you?" No words could even attempt to come out since I had to hold my breath.

I needed to take a deep breath, but there was no room to inhale. I grabbed the door knob, closed my eyes, and braced for impact. This was a big wave, complete with the feeling that I was being stabbed with a knife in my vagina. Exhaling, I looked at him and rolled my eyes as he said, "Did you call the doctor?"

My thoughts were racing. Do I just kill him now or actually explain that I couldn't call the doctor because I can't move. I'm sure if I kill him, I would be covered by a temporary insanity plea. I can't risk another false alarm, so I quickly grab my watch and leave the bedroom after the contraction finally ended.

I can hear him saying, "I don't know what you want me to do. If the doctor wants us to go to the hospital, let me know." I continue to walk down the stairs, thinking, "Oh, I'll be sure to let you know, asshole." I'm full of anger right now, I just want to get in the car and drive way. "Oh baby inside, I am so sorry you have such an inconsiderate ass for a dad."

I track another four contractions, then I have an uncontrollable urge to pee. Thank God I had to pee because that definitely brought some relief.

I wash my hands and await another contraction, but nothing. I walk into the kitchen and pour a much needed glass of water. All is quiet. Ten

minutes go by, nothing. I want to go back to sleep
but the fear of waking up next to him during a
contraction makes my skin crawl.

I sit on the couch staring at the unlit candles
on the fireplace. I contemplate lighting them and
saying a prayer, but I'm too exhausted. I rub my
belly as I feel her move into a more comfortable
position. I wish I could move into a more
comfortable position. Another five days and maybe I
can sleep on my belly. I suppose I will actually miss
being pregnant, because at least now there's quiet,
but oh I want my body back.

All right, it has now been an hour, and no
contractions, so I head back to bed. My husband
doesn't flinch as I roll into my nest of pillows. My
heart is racing from the walk up the stairs and, as
soon as I catch my breath, I'm out for two hours
straight.

I'm not sure if I woke up on my own or if the
hiccups from within startled me, but she has them
again. I move to my side in an attempt to give her
more room, but that seems to make me need to pee.

I make my first attempt to roll out of bed.
Some days it takes about three or four attempts. On

my second attempt, I feel a forceful hand on my back. My husband is helpful at pushing me toward the wall so I can use it for leverage to get up. I had him move our bed at an angle over a month ago. The bed looks like an island floating in the center of the room with my side inches from the wall. I use the wall to stabilize my balance as I not so gracefully stumble to my feet.

Before heading to the bathroom, I grab for my phone, which had alerted me earlier of a text, but I couldn't reach it from my position on the bed. I edge over and pick it up. Before I read the text, I notice the date. Today is my grandmother's birthday. I obviously hope this baby and she will share a birthday, but neither of them have ever been good at sharing. Over the years, my grandmother would tell me stories of her youth, only to have me asking for more details and she just wouldn't share them. She shared what she liked at the time...only what she wanted to share.

This granddaughter inside seems to take after her. She will share herself with the world on her terms. No pre-birth facial photo, no on-time arrival, and no hint of her name.

The text is a reminder of the arrival time for inducement. My doctor is pretty tech-savvy. It's helpful to get these reminders. Well, I really am five days away from the formal eviction of this child. I can't believe I will have to be induced. I should have bought those smokes the other day.

Speaking of shopping, I did go to the mall yesterday for three hours. I didn't plan to stay for that long, but, by the time I walked the length of the mall and wanted to leave, I realized I would have to walk all the way back to my car.

I purposely stopped at the Children's' Place to peek in the nursing room and got a little nap! My girlfriends told me about these secret mothers' stations. The Children's Place and The Gap are the only ones in my mall that have special stalls for nursing mothers—both complete with changing stations. These stops, according to my experienced breast-feeding mom friends, are the places to go if you don't want to whip a boob out in public. I planned to be discreet, so I'm glad they shared this secret with me.

One of my friends told me about the time she nursed in the changing room at Ann Taylor, only to be told they prefer babies not be changed or nursed in their stalls. She did tell me that Macy's has more comfortable changing stations if you opt for the larger dressing room.

I was glad to see that no one was in the station, so I snuck in and got a thirty-minute rest. I so badly wanted to elevate my feet and curl up in a ball, but neither were options for this body. Both the baby and I needed this rest. She slept, or at least didn't move while I rested, checked emails, and text my husband.

He offered to meet me for lunch in an hour. I told him that if I wasn't at the restaurant, then to come peel me out of the nursing station stall in The Children's Place. I set my iPhone timer for twenty minutes so that if I did nod off, I would wake in time to make the walk for lunch.

The thought of lunch was exciting as I hadn't eaten since the hardboiled egg at breakfast. I had packed a snack, but I ate that while driving to the mall, which was only about twenty minutes after breakfast. This baby would require food soon.

It was a good thing I set my timer so I appeared to be gathering my bags together when a new mother came in with her newborn and a two-year-old. She smiled at me and asked, "When are you due?"

"Any moment," I said.

She attempted to say something to me, but her two-year-old was nagging her for a snack as she was setting up to give the baby a bottle. She had her hands full, reaching for some packaged Goldfish crackers for one kid and shaking a bottle for the other, all while taking the baby out of the stroller that was balanced with her shopping bags. The stroller would have flipped sideways if she hadn't had the instinct to throw a knee on one side.

She kissed her baby and gestured for her two-year-old to sit next to me as she settled into her seat. "It will be over soon, and it gets easier," she told me.

I just smiled and packed up my packages. Easier? Maybe for her since she seemed to have an extra limb that I couldn't see. Hopefully I'll get that after I give birth. Right now, I really just wanted lunch. I was tempted to ask for a few Goldfish crackers, but I just smiled and said, "Thanks."

The walk to the restaurant wasn't so bad. I selected the nearest restaurant for fear that I couldn't make it within the half hour, which turned out to be perfect timing to walk there on time. It didn't take me a half hour to walk there but it did allow me to make a few purchases before I left the store. I just had to buy more clothes!

My husband chuckled as he watched me waddle in with my bags. "What did you buy now?" he asked, rolling his eyes.

"Oh I got the cutest matching outfits for the girls." I whipped out a peach gingham dress with a matching hat for the baby and a Capri pant outfit for her sister.

"Nice," he said.

"That Children's Place has the cutest clothes and it's so hard to find matchy outfits for a newborn and a six-year-old, so I had to get this other outfit, too." I proceed to take out two matching jean dresses with coordinating hats and shoes. "I hope the shoes will fit, I have no idea what size to buy."

He smiled and shook his head. He is just as excited to have girls in matching outfits, but doesn't say anything. At least that is what I think he is thinking.

The waitress brought us over two glasses of ice water. By the time she came back to take our order, I had finished all of mine and half of his. Everything on the menu looked good, but I decided on soup and salad because I knew that, if I went into labor in the next forty-eight hours, I wanted to have something light and easy to throw up.

As my husband talks, the baby wakes up. She definitely knows his voice and she is squirming for attention. He's a little annoyed that I'm not paying attention to what he's saying.

"Are you listening?" he asks.

"I'm trying," I say. "This little girl won't stop moving around." At that moment, he puts his hand on my belly and she kicks him.

"Wow, she's strong," he says.

"What she is, is stubborn!" I say. "She needs to get out and stop playing games."

"I know; I'm anxious to see her, too. Be patient."

"Patient?" I say, as I adjust my rib cage so her foot won't get stuck. "That's easy for you to say. I have to do all the work to get her out, and I'm tired now. It's not fair that I have to be patient while she's having a party inside me."

He laughs and says, "She's not having a party. And you'll be fine. It will be over soon."

"Ugh, that is the second time I heard that today. 'It will be over soon,' well not soon enough and you better make sure I get that epidural on time. Like today."

"Five days is the most you'll have to wait," he reminds me. "Do you have any other names we should discuss?"

I roll my eyes and look at my belly. "Come on kiddo, just tell us your name and come out already."

Lunch was nice except that I kept dropping my lunch on my belly. Just lovely, now I'll have to walk around the mall with salad dressing stains on my shirt, and crumbs itching me in my bra. I tried to use my napkin, but that kept dropping on the floor.

It is par for the course for me to drop things. Each day when my husband gets home from work, he finds lots of things on the floor. I just leave the stuff I drop, tissues, spoons, mail, etc and let him pick it up because I'm DONE bending over!

A few months ago, I could squat and pick up the items. When it became impossible to squat and get up without help, I began to pick things up with my toes. I would bend my knee almost as far as my butt and then reach around to get the item. That hasn't happened in weeks now; mostly because I lose my balance, so I just leave the stuff I drop on the floor!

Thank God we have a dog. He takes care of any food I spill or drop. He will probably miss me being pregnant most of all, but with two kids in the house, I'm sure there will be more than enough scraps to clean up.

## 4

# *Siding & Other Jobs*

My feet stink today; yet another wonderful pregnancy plus. I showered, but they still stink. I squirted lotion on the floor and rubbed my feet in it. But then I rubbed the lotion off when I used my feet to clean the lotion off the floor with a towel. Naturally, I left the towel on the floor. Someone will pick it up later. It certainly won't be me.

I went downstairs and asked my daughter to smell my feet. "Really Mom, smell your feet?" she said, sarcastically.

"Yes, you said they stunk this morning when you crawled in bed with me, so at least you can tell if they are improved."

Having a six-year-old roll her eyes at you is kind of funny. I would have told her it wasn't polite, but she was leaning down to smell my feet, and asking someone to smell your feet, isn't the most polite thing to do either.

"Nope, they stink," she said, as she pretended to pass out.

Feeling defeated, I said. "Well, they are clean." I explained that I attempted to put lotion on them, saying, "At least my slippers fit today so I'll keep them on and stay away."

"Ahem," she said. "Did you forget to say something to me?"

Feeling proud that she knows when manners should be used, I said, "Thank you," even if I did have her smell my feet. I kissed her on the head and thought about going back upstairs to spray perfume on my feet, but the journey downstairs was enough for now.

Today was Saturday and what would be a better thing to do than to go into labor. My husband said he had some errands to run for work, so I gladly got into his truck for a bumpy ride. We went to the grocery store in search of G2 grape-flavored, but they were out. We stopped at his office to check on a fax that didn't arrive, and we planned to quickly run into the pet shop for dog bones, but got distracted by dog toys and forgot the bones.

He is now watching TV and relaxing, while I'm sweeping the porch. Another energy burst, I guess. I try to rearrange the rocking chairs on the porch, but I cannot move them as my belly is in the way. The baby is resting quietly with all my commotion. As I attempt to sweep another cobweb from the corner, I notice the siding is rather dirty.

Under the kitchen sink I have three new containers of Lysol Wipes. I learn quickly that one wipe cleans an entire forty-eight inches of siding really well. It looks so clean than I don't even realize I've gone through two containers until I reach for the third. Mental note, I need more wipes.

The porch and the siding look good. I can't reach the top six slats, but they aren't as dirty as the ones near the floor that I had to get on all four to clean for the past half-hour. My husband comes outside and sees the mound of dirty wipes. "What the heck are you doing?" he asks. Why does he ask such obvious questions?

"Just tidying the porch," I say.

"Get inside. You are supposed to take it easy," he says, as he easily bends over and picks up all the wipes. Holding the door open, he follows me inside with the trash. I immediately begin washing my very dry and dirty hands.

"I was hoping my water would break," I said, laughing.

He says, "Something better break soon before you go completely insane and start cutting the grass with scissors."

He is so funny. I am laughing so hard that I feel myself pee. "Oh no," I say as I run quickly to the bathroom.

"Did your water break?" he asks, standing in the doorway watching me trying to wipe myself from behind, which is no longer possible as my hand can't reach. I quickly wipe from the front hoping not to give myself an infection

"No, just peed a little. You can't make me laugh like that."

"It's not my fault you have a weak bladder," he says.

"Really? I believe this entire thing is your fault. This baby is the one that peed, not me and she wouldn't be peeing in me if you didn't put her there."

"Oh yeah, it was all my fault," he says, knowing he shouldn't try to argue this with me based on the serious look on my face.

"Do you want new pants or just new granny panties?" he asks.

"Just underwear, thank you. Pick out a sexy pair."

Underwear gets less sexy after the second trimester. I said I would never wear full granny panties, but the low rider bikinis didn't do much for belly protection. I had to graduate to some briefs just to keep the baby warm and to help support my belly muscles.

I changed and got comfortable…well clean, then headed into the kitchen to drink two huge glasses of water. My husband resumed watching his golf match and, well, I decided to sneak back to the porch with the Windex.

I proceeded to Windex all the windows on the porch, and the sliders. Then I moved onto taking the screens out. The dog looked at me in awe as I sprayed the screens with the hose. Thank goodness it's sunny out, the screens dried quickly, but I had to ask my husband to help put them back in. I could tell he didn't approve of my labors, but he knew not to say anything.

Everything looked great. I headed upstairs to take a well-deserved nap.

About eight minutes into my nap, the baby decided to move around. I guess I should know by now that, when I stop moving, she starts to move. Note to self, after delivery when she naps, so will I.

My nap didn't work out as I planned, but it was nice to have my daughter come snuggle with me. She laughed when she saw that the baby was aggravating me. At one point she said, "Baby sister, this is your big sister and I want you to kick mommy." And she did!

Sister-bonding seemed to have begun while one was still in the womb. They both ganged up on me. One would talk and the other apparently listened. I asked my daughter to tell her sister to settle down, but baby inside must have known it was *my* request and she didn't obey. I joked with both of them and said, "This little one is going to be punished until she is five or six for not listening to me."

*Angela Grout*

# 5

# *Fire Drills*

It's now 12:30 am. I woke up to pee and saw blood in the toilet. Not a lot, but enough to make me worry. I can't remember; is blood in your pee a sign of your water breaking? I head downstairs, but not before grabbing the labor basket I assembled the day after my husband didn't understand my wrist pointing command to time a contraction.

The basket contains a pad of paper, a pen, a clock, a bottle of water, the cordless phone, my *What to Expect when You're Expecting Book*, and my doctor's phone number. I figured I would have all the essentials together in case of a moment like this.

I sat waiting for contractions to start, but nothing. I tried to get the baby to move, but nothing. She is sleeping very soundly. And she is pressing on my lungs right now! I'm having a hard time breathing. And actually my ass hurts, too. What the heck!

After evaluating my symptoms: bleeding, neck ache, breathing issues, ass pain, a very heavy belly, I decide this has to be labor, unless I'm having a heart attack. There are so many issues to make me believe that I could really be in labor, but then again, it could be so many things, including a false alarm. And I don't know if I can rule out heart failure, as my heart is beating out of my chest and I certainly can't breathe very well! The main issue is, I'm not having any contractions, and the baby isn't moving. Fear begins to overwhelm me.

After an hour of allowing my thoughts to race, I decide to call the doctor. It takes about ten minutes for Doc to return my call.

Doc says not to worry. If I want to head to the hospital I can, but he thinks I should wait until I have some painful contractions. Not that I want painful contractions, but it seems if I had at least one contraction, then it would be easier to justify waking my husband. I don't want to make my mother come over in the middle of the night only to be sent home for another "false alarm."

It is very confusing to know WHEN to go to the hospital. I pretty much have had contractions since January and often they were three-to-four minutes apart, but now, with no contractions and just these aches, I don't know. I have had too many false alarms over the past three weeks.

Only eight days ago, Doc said I would deliver within the week. Then last week, the nurse said it would be by the end of last weekend. Now this week, nothing. I am beginning to think it will never happen! OOOH...Ouch! It has to be today! This mystery needs to have an ending NOW!

One part of the mystery is over and that is that this baby will be a Pisces like her dad. The only way she wouldn't be a Pisces is if I give birth in three weeks. There is no possibility of that since my inducement day is two days away. Any way I look at it, I will have this baby out within the next forty-eight to seventy-two hours.

Next thing I know the sun is waking me up. I'd fallen asleep in the glider and actually got some rest. It's now 5:51 am, the baby is stretching and making me have to urgently pee.

There are no signs of any contractions and, with the baby moving around, I feel more confident that all is normal and well. The aches I'm having are probably unrelated to labor, but more likely caused by all the cleaning I did yesterday. My neck, wrists, and even my shoulders are sore. My belly feels so hard and my back is killing me. Guess I shouldn't have been on all fours cleaning the porch because I'm literally out of shape.

The bleeding from last night only occurred that one time; I am beginning to think I imagined it. Thank goodness the baby is moving, so I know she's okay. My belly is so hard. I almost feel as though I'm having a contraction, but it isn't as much the pain I am feeling, it's the pressure. An intense pressure, like there is a balloon inflated inside me and wants to rupture.

I begin to rub my belly and hope that it will relax. However, between the tightness and the baby moving, I'm very uncomfortable. I use all my energy to get upstairs to sit on my birth ball. I remember that bouncing on the birth ball helped to relieve a similar sense of pressure last month, so I bounce next to my bed and read a book, hoping to get my mind off what is going on.

My daughter comes into the room and knocks on my belly. "Good morning, Sis, are you coming out today?" she asks.

Ugh, a thump, swoosh and a little more inflation of the balloon. I try to catch my breath, but it seems the baby is stretched into my lung cavity and isn't allowing me room to inhale as deeply as I need to.

"I hope so," I said.

My husband sits up as he hears me tell my daughter that I called the doctor last night and they said I could go to the hospital anytime I want now.

"Well, let's go, then," he says.

"I don't know. I don't want to be sent home again. I really haven't had any contractions, just intense pressure and a bad back ache which is probably from cleaning yesterday. And don't even say I told you so," I warn him.

The three of us watch Sesame Street and I send telepathy to the baby. "Okay little one, if you want to come out today, just give me two or three contractions and we'll go, otherwise I will wait until my appointment on Tuesday."

Well, she listened and the contractions started within the hour. By 9:30, I had my husband drop our daughter off to my mom and we were on our way. Once we checked in, I began to think about the date. "Honey, next year on this day we will be having a birthday party. How cool is that?"

My husband looked at me and said, "Just relax and push this girl out before you go ordering her party favors. Just get through this right now."

Oh how he knows me. If I could distract myself and get on my iPhone right now, then I could go to Amazon.com and begin ordering those party favors. I wonder if she will want a flower theme party or if she'll like a particular character, and I'll have to purchase the entire collection to decorate with. My iPhone is in my bag and I don't think asking my husband to get it would be a smart idea right now.

The nurses put my wristband on and inform me that the doc will check me in a few minutes. I pray I am fully dilated. Please God let this go quick, I think.

Doc checks me and I am only two centimeters dilated. Same as I was over two months ago. How is that possible? I've had at least one hundred contractions and I want this baby out! Doc says she can start some Pitocin now or I can go home and continue natural labor there. When the contractions get really bad, I can come back. I don't know what to do.

"Can I get an epidural now?" I ask.

Doc says no, not until I am five or six centimeters.

"How soon will that be?"

"There are no guarantees. If you want, go home where you are comfortable, and let nature take its course. I will set up an office appointment for you tomorrow. If I set up that appointment, you surely won't need it."

My husband chimed in and said, "Remember how slow delivery was the first time on the Pitocin, maybe this time if you labor at home, it will be quicker."

"Okay," I said, discouraged to be leaving the hospital with another false alarm.

We picked up our daughter and headed home on a beautiful sunny day. I rocked on the porch as I watched her attempt to learn to ride a two-wheeler. After about an hour, I went inside and took a nap.

Contractions woke me up, but they were mild compared to what I have experienced so far, so I just laid in bed. With each contraction I thought about how toned my stomach muscles should be. Maybe after delivery I won't have to work at getting six pack abs. That would be a plus to all this contracting.

My husband came to check on me just as I was thinking about taking a shower. "How are you doing?" he asks.

"I'm okay. A few little contractions, but nothing stopping me dead in my tracks like before," I say. As I roll out of the nest of pillows and catch myself on the wall, he comes over and helps me the rest of the way up.

"Do you smell smoke?" I ask.

He rolls his eyes. "There is no smoke. Go take your shower."

Smelling smoke is another pregnancy quirk I have had continually throughout this pregnancy and the last. It prevents me from being able to breathe and makes me feel like I am being choked by cigarette smoke or, sometimes smoke from an electrical fire. My poor husband has had to check the house out for fire on several occasions, following me like a dog as I have my nose in the air searching for the root of the scent.

He has ignored my request to search for fire over the past few months. One of my friends says that maybe it's my grandparents' spirit around me. My grandparents did smoke, so maybe it's Holy Smoke surrounding me and protecting me. If it's not a fire and if it's not my grandparents, then the only other explanation is this baby is overdone and I am smoking inside!

My shower was great. I did a special conditioning treatment for my hair and I was able to hold my breath long enough to shave part of my legs. Quite an accomplishment. I wish I felt more comfortable about asking my husband to shave my legs and prep me for delivery, but I don't think I could have him do that. I have a girlfriend who had her husband shave her weekly during her pregnancies, but it kind of gives me the willies.

I attempted to blow dry my hair, but with the baby all excited about the shower, she was trying to move around and it was making me nauseous. The doctor had given me a sleeping pill and told me I could take it. She said often real labor will wake you up, and that the more I slept the more relaxed I would be so I would dilate.

I took the pill, since having a glass of wine wasn't an option.

# 6

# *Tumor or Tomorrow*

I slept all afternoon yesterday. I even slept all night last night with the help of another Ambien. I am having some mild contractions this morning and my appointment is in an hour, to be followed with an ultrasound and then a consultation at one. I hope I am eight centimeters and can be admitted. I hope I only have to push twice and by four she will be delivered. (I can dream can't I?)

I double checked my hospital bag; it's been packed for three months. Bathrobe, tooth brush, slippers, new nursing pajamas, underwear, nursing sports bra, and clothes for the baby. I packed the baby two outfits. The newborn outfit is a simple onesie in purple and the other is slightly bigger and it's pink with an elephant on the chest. I secretly hope I can use the pink elephant outfit because I bought her a pink stuffed elephant to snuggle with. The elephant is embroidered, *Mommy loves you.*

I have a separate bag for labor supplies, including chap stick, body lotion, hand cream, saltine crackers, a deck of cards, a pad of paper, a pen, a tennis ball for rolling on my back (in the childbirth classes, they indicated that a ball could be helpful), and a bag of lollipops to suck on (no lifesavers, as I could choke on them). Lollipops have a handle so I can hold the handle and pull it out if I have a sudden contraction that creates me to suck in unintentionally. (Another lesson from childbirth classes.)

I packed a change of socks, a spray bottle, in case I need to be misted, and a photo of my daughter and my dog.

I also have in my bag, a change of clothes for my husband, along with three magazines, two Gatorades, and a pack of trail mix in case he needs a snack. I know he wouldn't pack himself a bag, but, on the chance that labor is long and he is hungry or bored, at least I have something for him. I highly doubt he will need a change of clothes because I know he won't stay the night. He will have to go home to let the dog out, so I hope I can get this baby out and leave enough time for the dog and him to have some quiet time.

I did, of course, already ask my in-laws to come and let the dog out and feed him, but I know my husband will want to sleep in his own bed and, having to check the dog is the perfect excuse to leave me and the baby at the hospital. Perhaps that is when he will meltdown with the realization that life is forever changed again.

Knowing that he is returning home before I do is helpful so that if I need any supplies he can get them. I already put a different outfit for me to wear home on my chair, just in case I lose so much weight during delivery that the pants I brought are too big.

My appointment is in an hour.

"Oh please, please please let me be fully dilated."

The thought of having to wait until tomorrow for inducement is absurd. Why this baby isn't coming out is baffling. Oops, she heard that, and is trying to wriggle around, however there is no room. I inhale as deeply as I can to make my rib cage go higher and give her more room. It doesn't help; it just gets me winded.

My belly is tightening nonstop. If this is a contraction, it hasn't let loose all morning. I need to find the belt around my belly and cut it off. I am trying to take my mind off being so uncomfortable by rereading my baby journal. The poor journal is so messy. For my other daughter, I kept a neat, organized journal but for this baby, it is just scrap papers and pictures thrown into a box.

I take ten minutes and put the notes in chorological order. I wouldn't want this baby to come out and feel less loved than my first because her journal is so messy. Now it looks relatively neat enough so that I can continue her story after she is born. Truth be told, the second child does get less attention during pregnancy. I didn't want it to happen, but life gets busy and, well, I guess I got lazy.

OOOHHH…well that was a nice painful contraction. I have that awful knife feeling in my vagina. What the heck is that? The birth ball seems to be my only refuge when I get that feeling. I have already asked if I can bring it to the hospital, but they informed me I can request one. I will.

The contractions are three-to-five minutes apart now. I'm thankful that we are leaving for the hospital soon as the last one was a real nail-biter. My back is killing me, and I have the worst clamp or cramp around my entire belly EVER. My whole body aches. If it wasn't for the heavy action in my crotch, I would think I was getting the flu. I wish I could just roll onto my belly and curl into a ball, but just getting up from the birthing ball is enough motion.

My iPod is playing "Breathe" which has pretty much been my mantra song all pregnancy. Having to remember to breathe has probably been one of my most difficult chores. There is no room to inhale or exhale. OUCH, I swear this kid has weapons in there.

I close my eyes and concentrate on the song while holding my breath during the contraction. I peek at the time and its 11:09, when the contraction ends it is 11:11. Lucky number for me. Eleven-eleven has always been the number I was taught as a child to make a wish on, so I do. "I wish for this baby to get out today." Ouch, another contraction, it's still 11:11. Ugh. They can't be this close together. I exhale as my muscles release and see it is still 11:11. Amazing how time can stop forever for just a second.

I change my iPod song to "11:11." That's the song my cousin wrote and recorded years ago. She has a beautiful acoustic voice and I was listening to that song at her first concert when I went into labor with my first daughter, so maybe it will help to get this baby out.

I can hear my husband on the phone while in route to the doctor's office. "We have an appointment at 11:30; if she isn't getting admitted then I will be in this afternoon. Check on that Hall Street fire and don't forget to send the estimate to HUD. I'll call in an hour when I know more."

He is talking to his office manager. Isn't that special? He's going in to work if I don't have this baby, and leave his dying wife at home as he ventures into the real world and forgets the pain I'm in. If only there was a way to install a device for him to have this same pain. We should be experiencing this together. I know we are having a baby together, but this is all me right now. None of this affects him in any way, except for the argument I want to pursue.

I can't argue, I can't even talk. What the heck is squeezing my stomach so tight that I can't move? My hands are clutching the rollover handle above the door, and my feet are braced for sudden impact. I wish I could scream, but silence is all I can manage in my struggle for air. All the breathing exercises I learned during childbirth class are useless. I wish I was a stronger swimmer, because if I could hold my breath longer, then I would be fine. Each time I hold my breath, I barely have enough time to exhale and inhale again before the next contraction.

My husband looks at me and says, "You better write down the times of those contractions."

"Really?" I think. "Oh yeah, I'm on that, buddy." Thank God I can't talk, because I seriously want to kill him. "You write it down asshole, I'm a little busy trying to stay alive right now."

It will be great when I finally get strapped to a monitor, then the contractions will be real to him. Each time I have been in the hospital and had a contraction while attached to the monitor, he enjoys seeing how strong they are. I admit it is cool because then I know it is real and not some phantom pain. I still wonder if this is a phantom pregnancy. What if I really do have a tumor like I suspected from the beginning. Have they every confused a baby with a tumor?

Actually that has happened. I had a tumor when I was thirteen and, when they removed it, they seemed to think it was my twin. Seriously, that is what they think. I had a dermoid cyst and it contained hair, teeth, bones, and other particles to make a baby. Studies show that a dermoid cyst contains the leftovers from what should have been a baby, but was neglected proper nutrients. I must have needed her nutrients and took them from her. How generous of her to share. As in the movie *Pitch Perfect*, "I ate my twin in the womb."

If this baby inside me has eaten her twin, then she has to weigh over twenty pounds. This would be helpful in my own weight loss.

OOOOH…that was another good one. The speed bump into the hospital garage parking lot must have caused that one. "Sorry," says my husband.

"I'm fine," I say. That one actually was really quick.

I'm so happy I got a good night's sleep last night. That Ambien was a life saver. I wonder if Doc will give me more so I can get a good night's sleep again within the next eighteen or thirty years. My husband could use it today. He slept with our daughter last night because he said I was snoring. That just goes to show you that I slept soundly.

My poor daughter was not happy to find him in her bed because he messed up the sheets and threw some pillows on the floor. She is a little bit of a neat freak, which I'm sure I will appreciate as she gets older, but watching her have a breakdown over pillow misplacement at six years old and at 6:45 in the morning is tough!

*Angela Grout*

# 7

# *Order Up*

"What is taking so long?" I ask my husband as I quietly begin a trance into a picture in the doctor's waiting room. We arrived over fifteen minutes ago and all I can think about is how badly I want my birth ball to sit on.

The two sets of stairs and the five hundred feet we had to walk from the car to the doctor's office seemed to kick these contractions up a notch. Stopping in the stairwell, clutching the rail, I patiently waited the wave out. I informed the gals at the front desk that I'm having contractions and they can see me through the window, which I am contemplating smashing.

There is only one other person besides us in the waiting room. My husband tells me to sit. I give him the look of death. I have one leg on the chair in hopes that spreading my legs will make the baby fall out and then the girl at the front desk will believe that I need to be seen NOW.

The picture is nice, it has a ship and I think I see fish, or maybe it's a house and those are cows. I can't concentrate on the picture. How can people focus on a picture and forget all pain...not me. OOOUUUCH! I am screaming inside. My saving grace at this moment is that there's no way I am going home. I have to have this baby today.

After what seemed to be a five-minute-long contraction, I turn to my husband and say, "I want an epidural, now, please."

He smiles at me, knowing there is nothing he can say to help me.

The door opens and I see a medical salesman displaying a platter of sandwiches in the interior office. "Oh my God," I think. "They better not have a lunch break before I get in there."

I'm certainly not having lunch today. Even if I wanted it, there's no way it would fit, nor could I swallow anything other than air right now. The food smells good and my husband says, "Maybe we can get lunch after this."

I try to tell him what I was thinking, but the belly band grabs hold of me so snuggly that I can't breathe. I stare ahead at the painting on the wall, counting. I do that a lot—just count. I count my steps when I walk and I often find myself waking up counting in my sleep. I must have been a countess in a past life.

I hear myself say "forty-five" and the nurse opens the door and tells me I can come in.

Obviously, she is trained in spotting women in labor, as she says to me, "Do you think you can walk in now, or do you want to wait a minute?"

I love her. "I'm okay, but I won't have long," I say.

"How long have the contractions been like this?"

"For three months," I say.

She laughs. "I mean today."

"All morning they were three-to-four minutes apart, but the last hour or so has been…" I can't finish as my uterus must know I'm here to have a baby.

The nurse helps me to breathe. She counts and breathes with me. This is helpful.

"You can't hold your breath," she says, like she thinks I forgot. Little does she know that holding my breath has been my coping mechanism.

"Take smaller, quicker breaths," she instructs.

Why the heck didn't I get a coach? Seriously, I want my husband to be present for the baby's birth, but as a coach, he certainly hasn't been very effective. Coaches are important. Then again, I am sure if he did tell me how to breathe, I would probably just get mad. At least this nurse is a woman and has, most likely, been through this since she seems to know what she's talking about.

She takes me straight to the ultrasound room. "We can do your exam in here and do the ultrasound too. I won't make you walk down the hall."

I really do love her. How thoughtful. "Can I get an epidural now?"

She smiles and says, "Well let's just see where we are at."

In between contractions, we discuss my flu-like symptoms. She says she would like to do the ultrasound between contractions to make sure the baby is face down and then have the doctor check me for dilatation.

"That's fine," I say, having never been more excited to have fingers inside me. I actually feel giddy. "Let him check, I think I'm ten centimeters, and I want to get this baby out now."

She puts the cold gel on my belly. Maybe the coldness will bring down the swelling. She notices me attempt to go into a trance as my crotch burns and my belly tightens. This is a long one. She's talking to me, but I can't hear her. I see my husband talking to her. I just need to breathe. She starts with the counting and I listen. My breath matches her counts and then it's over.

"Okay," she says, "I'm going to get the doctor, now. I don't deliver babies so it's best that I get him." That didn't sound like a joke. "The baby's head is down and she looks fine."

"How big do you think she is?" I ask, in an attempt to judge how much I'll have to push.

"About six or seven pounds. Perfect size."

My husband asks, "Do you think she'll be born today?"

"Oh yeah. I am going to call for a room now. I'll be right back."

I start to cry. I'm overcome with panic.

Oh my God, this is going to happen! I begin to pant. My husband tries to count, but I say, "I'm not having a contraction now, I just...sob, sob, snort, sob...don't know how I'm going to get her out."

"You'll be fine. You can do this."

"I don't know. I want to *not* do this. I want another option."

He laughs. "There is no other option. You will be fine. It will be over very soon and we'll finally see our daughter."

I consider arguing that I want him to push her out. She needs to get out! I can't breathe again. Only now the tightness in my uterus is equaled to my anxiety of pushing.

The doctor walks in smiling. "Guess we are going to have a baby today!" he says.

I pray out loud to everyone in the room, "Oh please tell me I'm ten centimeters and she'll slide out now."

The nurse holds my hand and counts my breaths as my husband watches the doctor check my cervix. It's amazing how, when you're pregnant these terms come so natural. If you asked me, outside of pregnancy, what my cervix felt like or how to check it, I would have no idea. Today I'm an expert at dilatation sizes and cervical tenderness.

He checks me and begins typing a lot into the computer. The silence is deadly. My husband finally breaks the silence and asks, "Is she more than two centimeters?"

Doc replies, "You are four centimeters."

WHAT??! I am so disappointed. How could that be? All this progress for only four centimeters? It's taken me three months to get this far. I'd better dilate another six centimeters within the hour and have her out before school gets out.

"I just ordered you an epidural," Doc says.

The sky opens and my eyes well with joyful tears. As I hear angels singing, I ask politely, "Can I get it now?"

"By the time you get to your room, it should be there."

"Within the hour?" I say, sounding discouraged. "What if I miss the opportunity?"

"You will be fine." Says Doc.

"But, Doc… If I dilate too fast, I could miss the opportunity to get an epidural! Can I get it now?"

"Sorry. I can't do it here. I don't have it here in the office."

"Can't you promise you can just get the baby out within the hour?"

"Maybe. But it probably be a few more hours. Let's just get you comfortable."

"Okay," I say. I need that. I need to be comfortable. I need to be able to breathe. I'm glad I packed magazines and playing cards. "Can I get a birth ball?"

The nurse says she will check on that for me.

My husband and I are alone in the room. He reaches for my hand to help me up off the little table, and I burst out crying.

"It's okay, honey. It will be fine." He asks, "Why are you crying?"

Huh…anxiety. I take a deep breath but I feel a panic attack coming on as I embrace the fact that I really will have to push soon. The switch has flipped and my tears won't stop flowing.

"Come on, it will all be over soon. You're going to be great. We can finally meet this little six-pounder and she can meet her sister."

I cry harder. This is happening. I can't stop it. I am both relieved that it will be over soon and she will be out, but petrified to have to do all the work.

# 8

# *Five Toe Curl*

We've been in the birthing room for over an hour. The epidural fairy has not arrived yet. I am trying to be patient, but I REALLY want it. The nurses told me to walk the hall, but I couldn't make it out of the room without freezing in place.

There is no birth ball option, either. Even if I had one, I couldn't use it because, now that I'm on the contraction monitor, I have to be in bed.

My husband is reading the magazines as the machine beeps incessantly. He watched the first few contractions on the monitor. That got old fast.

I can't do anything but stare and hold on. Each wave is quicker than the last. I call it a wave because my girlfriend told me that she imagined her contractions to be like a wave in the ocean. Coming in and then going out. I'm trapped in sand and, when the water comes in, I hold my breath waiting for the water to return back to the ocean. I must be in a typhoon because the air breaks are hard to find.

I loosen my grip on the bed rail just enough to adjust my grip when another wave comes. I silently vow not to let go again. The breaks are quick and the pressure is explosive. I'm convincing myself that each one is dilating me a centimeter at a time. I have to be close to ten now.

Every time the nurse comes in, I ask if I can get checked. She just says she will ask, but apparently she didn't ask the last time or the time before that. She just marks the paper on the machine and adjusts my belt. She obviously would prefer me on my back, but I can't get there. The cord from the machine is tangled between me, the bedrail, and the sheets. I take the cord from her and hold it in my grip. That should help to keep it untangled.

"Is the epidural fairy coming soon?" I ask, almost begging and commanding with distress.

"It's a busy day and he has one more downstairs," she says. "Then he will be here. I would guess within the half-hour."

Half-hour! My brain is calculating that if I have to wait half an hour and it takes half an hour to set up the epidural, then I may not get relief for another hour or even longer. At this rate, I won't be pushing this kid out until dinner time.

I'm not hungry, but I'm thinking about my husband who often forgets to eat. The poor guy will work all day and not eat, then come home and say it's too late to eat. No wonder he's so skinny. On the days I can't eat at work because it's busy, I eat double when I get home.

In between the next wave, I say, "Honey, if you want to go get something to eat, you might as well now, because by the time he gets here, the soonest I'll push is another hour or two."

He barely gives it a thought and begins packing up his magazine. While I'm glad for him, it seems a little unfair that he can leave this room and have a life, eat, and even stop to shop in the gift shop (which he should have done already). Me, well I just need to try staying alive—breathing, while ignoring the burning knife sensation in my crotch and the tightness in my chest.

Of course, as he kisses me goodbye, the door opens and the epidural cart is being pushed in. I should have sent him to lunch an hour ago! Well, at least I was nice and offered for him to leave.

I sign the consent form as the technician gets everything set up. He discusses the signal he will give me before he inserts the needle between contractions. The nurse is watching the machine in case I won't know when the contraction starts or ends.

The nurse and the technician are discussing the machinery. Apparently something is missing. The technician says he will be right back. I breathe my short breaths to control the contraction and my patience.

After the fourth contraction, I begin to doubt he is ever coming back. My husband watches the monitor and informs me that this contraction looks much stronger than the earlier ones. I nod and silently say, "Thanks honey, I couldn't tell!"

There's a knock on the door and then we hear some giggles. Two of my girlfriends are here. They snuck into the hospital, pretending to be spies and got into my labor and delivery room. I'm actually relieved to see them. They have both given birth, so maybe they will see that I'm being tortured.

"You're four centimeters and you haven't gotten an epidural yet?" says my friend Kate.

My husband explains that the technician had to get some part for the machine and left over fifteen minutes ago.

"Can you hook me up?" I ask her.

They all smile at me. Another contraction starts; they can tell by my face that I'm having one. Women are like that. They don't have to ask, "Are you having a contraction?" They know.

Kay holds my hand, while the three of them look at the monitor. "Wow, those are pretty strong and close together," she says. "When's the last time they checked you?"

I look at the clock and say, "Three hours ago. Do you want to check me?"

While I endure the labor pain, the three of them discuss that I could have this baby any minute. Both of my friends think I'm going to be fully dilated when the doctor checks me. I'm just concerned that I'm going to miss the opportunity for the epidural. If I don't get the epidural, I will have no rest before I have to devote all my time to being a mom to a newborn.

I plan to breastfeed, so most likely immediately after delivery I will try. I know it can be difficult for the first few latch-ons, and I really want to be patient and calm. Getting this epidural is my plan for staying calm. Once the epidural starts working, maybe I can discuss the baby's name, or at least discuss with the nurses how soon I can breastfeed.

My goal is to breastfeed for at least three months exclusively like I did for my firstborn. I'm hopeful to begin pumping soon so I can store up enough to give her a few feedings mixed with formula as I wean her to formula. I know that breast milk is best, and I really want to give her all the best nutrients to keep her healthy.

The nurses haven't even asked me yet if I plan to breastfeed, although I do remember writing it on the admission papers three months ago. They must know. I would ask, but with my eyes squeezed shut during this current contraction, all I can really do is pray for it to be over soon so I can ask, "Where is the damn epidural technician?"

I have one girlfriend who opted not to have an epidural. I now realize she has a much higher threshold for pain than I do. She told me it was like a rollercoaster, going up, up, up in anticipation for the downward exhilarating breeze. There is nothing downward about this. I get the up, up, up, which is more like tighter tighter, tighter, but the downward exhilaration doesn't exactly happen like that. It's like a quick breeze and back to climbing an ever steeper hill.

My friends are watching the monitor and, once again, inform my husband that these contractions are bad and he should go find the nurse.

I love them.

Katie brought her camera and begins taking photos of the warming bed that is in the room, along with what I think is a picture of me mid-contraction.

I should ask her to take video when the birth happens, however, I really don't know if I want crotch shots or her focusing a lens there.

In the old days they used to set up a mirror so you could watch the birth, but I don't know how you would watch it when your eyes are squeezed shut from the constriction of labor pans. Then again if I get that epidural anytime soon, maybe I will ask for a mirror.

On second thought, watching myself give birth does not seem like an option for me, because if I see myself poop or even start to push a head out, I may pass out, myself. One of my greatest fears is pooping during delivery. My husband says I didn't the first time. This time, in preparation for this moment, I haven't really eaten a solid meal in days. I figured if I don't have anything in me, I can't poop.

There's a knock on the door. It's the doctor. He wants to check me. I'm so excited; this is it. I'd better be ten centimeters. Oh no. If I am, then I will have to push this baby out without an epidural. I'm not sure exactly what I want now.

Doc is surprised at how well I'm doing, "Five centimeters," he says.

"Are you kidding me?" I want to scream at him, but knowing that the sound of my own voice will probably create another wave of intense pain, I quietly say, "Do you think you can give me the epidural?"

He looks the machine over and notices the missing piece. He makes a call and, within ten minutes, the technician is in the room.

"I'm sorry for the delay," he says. "It has been a busy day and we just had twins delivered downstairs. It looks like you're ready for this epidural, eh?"

"Yeah, like three months ago," I respond sarcastically.

"All right, we need to get you sitting up. Do you think you can manage that? Let's try it after the next contraction."

I attempt to get up immediately. I'm not waiting. Let's get this show on the road! Just as I make the attempt, I'm hit with an iceberg. I'm not cold, but I certainly am frozen in place. Trying to take short breaths, and clenching the bedrail, I hear my husband, "In a few minutes you won't feel that anymore. You're doing great."

The second it ends, I reach for him with my left hand, while my right hand keeps a death grip on the bedrail just in case I get struck by a sword to the abdomen and need to hold on for dear life. He grabs my hand and uses his other to push my back and help me sit up. The force is almost barbaric, but it does work quickly. By the time I swing my legs around, the tube inside by belly expands with explosive pressure.

"Ahhhhhhhh" I exhale and open my eyes to see the technician holding a turkey baster with a needle on the end. "Not what I wanted to see," I gasp, quietly.

The girls laugh and I know that it really is what I want to see. I want to know this pain will subside any minute. Seeing the actual cocktail in hand is a bit intimidating, but it truly is magical that someone somewhere thought of this safe cocktail of medicine to alleviate childbirth pains.

In the old days, they probably gave the laboring woman many shots of whiskey. That's most likely why so many women died in childbirth, not from complications but drunkenness. I mean when would you stop and how would you concentrate? Thank God some doctor created this magical epidural. Numb the pain without hurting the baby or the mother.

The technician tells me that after the next contraction he will insert the line. Everyone watches the monitor; I can only see the piles of paper that it has spewed all over the floor. There are a lot of pointy lines that plunge back down and back up over and over again. I close my eyes not wanting to be reminded of where I have been.

As the contraction starts the downward fall on the monitor, I feel a pinch in my back. It's in. I feel relieved until I realize he's poking the needle around. I try counting; hoping that when I get to three it will be over. I get to two and hear, "I will try it again on the next contraction."

*Angela Grout*

# 9

# **Brad Pitt**

I can't even image how women give birth in a field, or in an airplane bathroom or even a bus terminal. How do you labor in public quietly and then just squat down, push a kid out, wrap a blanket around it, and go back to picking rice. I couldn't do it.

I really don't even see how you could be comfortable on a toilet in a bus station…never mind the cleanliness of the environment there, but being your own midwife? I read once where a woman in my town gave birth on her living room floor as she was waiting for the EMTs.

There is no way she had labor pains for days, weeks, or months like I did. How the heck did she gather towels, get scissors to cut the cord and prepare herself to catch the baby? On second thought, I think I remember reading that her four year old son helped her. I suppose he could have gathered the supplies, but seriously, how could she think clearly enough to know what to do?

My girlfriend who gave birth without the epidural and who described contractions like a wave, gave herself the mantra of, "My body will know what to do." What great faith she had. I suppose the lady that gave birth on her floor and the lady in the bus terminal also used that mantra. I tried it for my first daughter, but her labor was over forty hours long.

Yes I said it, forty hours of labor. I did have an epidural for most of it, however, it was much different than this labor. The pain wasn't intense. I woke up at home three days past my due date, went to the bathroom to pee and couldn't stop peeing. It didn't feel like pee because I had no control. I had been practicing Kegels all pregnancy, but not one Kegel stopped the flow.

I took an exercise class for pregnant women and, as one of the closing rituals, she would have us sit in a chair and do Kegels. The instructors name was Tiger. She would tell us to imagine our vagina as an elevator. We open the doors and move it up to each floor. She actually told us to imagine that Brad Pitt was getting in and we wanted to take him to the top floor. Once we were at the top, we would hold him prisoner until we slowly, very slowly descended to the ground floor to open the doors and let him out.

I didn't imagine Brad Pitt, I couldn't even imagine my husband. I did the exercise, but it grossed me out to know all the women might be imagining Brad in their vaginas. This was a New Age twist, I guess, to an old wives tale of strengthening the Kegel to make for easier labors.

When my water broke at home, I had called the doctor and he told me to head to the hospital. I woke my husband up to tell him, and he gathered all the bags. He was a little surprised when he came back in from loading the car and found me in the shower.

"What are you doing?" he asked, obviously irritated.

I explained that I had no contractions and felt great so I wanted to shower and shave and prepare myself for delivery. I planned to beautify myself. This time was different, all right. I just wanted this baby out.

For my first, as soon as I arrived at the hospital, they helped to get my labor to progress with an IV of Pitocin. After a full day, nothing happened. I had a few minor contractions, but spent most of the day playing cards with my husband, circling the nurses' station around one thousand times, and talking on the phone to my friends to pass the time. Needless to say, this time is different.

I checked in the hospital on December 1$^{st}$ for my first and gave birth to her on December 3$^{rd}$ at 12:10 am, after nine hours of pushing. Yes I said that!

I suppose all that pushing has given me a little anxiety about pushing this baby out. I was offered a C-section twice, but my doctor really felt that natural delivery would be best for a quicker recovery and I certainly wanted to enjoy my baby and not be worried about recovering from surgery.

I have had several surgeries in my life, including a C-section to remove that tumor caused from me eating my twin in the womb. I was thirteen when that particular tumor was removed. The doctors left me with a big zipper scar which has stopped me from ever becoming a stripper or living in a nudist colony.

That C-section surgery was very painful to recover from. I held a pillow to my stomach for about three weeks after the surgery and, when I got the staples out, I passed out. I remember thinking back then, if I had had a baby, how would I even hold it, let alone change it, or anything. I could barely walk without my guts spilling to the floor.

I'm glad I had a natural childbirth. I do remember that, as soon as she came into the world, all the labor pains instantly were gone. Well, except for when my uterus was shrinking back down to size, which they forget to tell you about in childbirth class. The nurses actually push on your belly so hard that you think your guts will rupture out like a squished caterpillar. Then for another two weeks, every time you breastfeed, your uterus will contract and you will hold your breath. I wish I had practiced more breath-holding techniques. I have to hold my breath through these contractions and I am fairly certain that if I don't get air soon, I will pass out.

"Okay, I'm in," says the technician.

I exhale and actually feel relief as I burp rather loudly. Burp, Burp, Burp again, oh my. I guess I'm full of gas. With each burp, I feel my belly add another brick to my crotch. This is the Willy Wonka experience without the fizzy lifting drink. The pressure on my vagina is heavy. This kid must have a thirty pound bowling ball smashing through my cervix.

"Do you feel any better?' asks Katie.

I assess myself, the pressure from my vagina is radiating into my lower back more ferociously than before. The belly band is choking me and I think I have a foot stuck in my rib cage again. "Ugh, maybe," I say, knowing I don't want to talk much until the cocktail takes effect. "Give me a few minutes."

Within seconds, I feel much better. The pressure is gone. My belly is still hard as a rock and I really would like it to relax, but overall I realize I can hold a conversation now.

# 10

## *Snack Break*

For over thirty minutes I enjoy pleasant conversation with my girlfriends. Which allowed my husband a mini break to get a bite to eat. They are vigilant at keeping me informed as to when I'm having a contraction by the results on the monitor. It really is amazing the relief that epidural provides.

Katie asks me if I have a name for the baby. I don't. I tell her I still like Lilliana but no one else does.

My husband comes into the room while we are having this conversation, and he chimes in with why he doesn't want Lilliana. The girls ask him for his favorites. I barely listen because I feel pressure down there. I must be imagining it, I must be just so mad that he is ignoring my Lilliana request that I'm now imagining pain again. I grab the bedrail and close my eyes.

"Are you okay?" Kay asks.

"Check the monitor, am I having a contraction?'

Katie looks over and examines the cash register roll of reports that has been spilling out. "Yup, not as bad as the ones an hour ago, but it was a good one."

"Yeah, I know." I turn to my husband who is looking at the epidural IV. "It's running," he says.

For what seems like another five hundred belly squeezes, I ask the nurse if I can turn up the medication. She points and says, "Just hit this button." I actually had been hitting it. Since nothing was working, I thought it was the nurses' station button. "I don't think it works," I say.

She examines the machine and informs me that it is working, but said she will call the technician.

Miraculously, he shows up almost immediately. He looks at the machine and says, "Some of these machines have been acting up. It looks okay." He is behind me so I cannot see him, but I look at my friends as they keep watch over what he's doing.

"Any better?" he asks.

When she notices me rolling my eyes and clutching the bedrail with my feet flexed to the sky, Katie says, "I don't think so."

"Well, there was a slight kink in the line, it should be fine now." He looks at his beeper and says, "I'll be back in ten minutes." And he leaves on a mission to save another life.

In the meantime, everyone goes back to the name-game discussion. I want to join in this time, as I really do want to have a name for the baby before she gets out. And I really want this baby out NOW!

OUUCH. I think my crotch just split open. I push my pain button to release more medicine. I actually push in five times. My husband looks at me and says, "You're doing fine."

"That epidural man better come back soon. I don't think this is working."

"It's working, I can see the bag flowing."

I feel clammy now, and nauseous, and I think I have to pee. Actually I really want to pee. And I need to burp. Oh those burps I had before were amazing. If only I could burp again and feel some release from this belly band. I ask my husband to take my socks off because my feet are swelling at an alarming and painful rate.

When he took my socks off, the nail polish on two of my toes came off from the sweat. I had just had them painted so they would look good during delivery. At least something was going to look pretty while I was in labor. Oh well, what a wasted pedicure!

I'm deep in thought when my cousin walks into the room.

"Hi, are you going to have this baby now or what?" She winks at me.

I smile as best as I can as I again, then brace for an impact. My right foot has found a new home on the cold part of the bedrail where the bar makes the T-shape. I can anchor my foot on that as I quietly control my breathing.

My cousin notices my naked toes. "Do you want me to paint your toes?"

She's always been good at making sure things look good. When our Memere was alive she would visit her on Sundays and do her hair, shave her face and paint her nails. It really is honorable to make someone feel good.

I whisper under the breath of the contraction, "I wish."

"Well your other foot looks good and your hair looks awesome."

I attempt to smile with my eyes squeezed closed causing the worst lines in my forehead. I will definitely need Botox after this.

"Didn't you get an epidural?" she asks, knowing full well I'm having a painful contraction.

"She has one," says my husband. "The guy just fixed the line, it was kinked so it should start working better for her now."

My cousin Wendy is the greatest. She is the closest thing I will ever have to a sister. We always said we would have our babies at the same time, but she started much earlier than me. Not because I didn't want to. I had some trouble conceiving. I struggled with endometriosis and that, most likely, caused my fertility issues.

Then again, endometrioses may have only played a small part in my difficulty to conceive. I have always wondered if the fact that I ate my twin also contributed. See, when they removed my twin's cyst, they also took my right ovary. And my theory was that if you ovulate each month from a different ovary, then I would ovulate every other month, or, at the least, I would run out of eggs quicker than average.

I think it was the latter that caused some of my inability to conceive on my own. For my first child, I was able to conceive only after the doctors put me on Clomid. With Clomid, I was able to harvest more eggs and, therefore, increase my chances of getting pregnant.

It's actually a longer story, but to make a long story short, which I'm not so good at, I will just say that I conceived my first with a little help from above.

Perhaps saying I had help from above is controversial since having help from above would mean that God, not a doctor, created my pregnancy.

I have great faith and I know God found me the doctors to help with my infertility. Whether or not I actually conceived with the help of drugs or doctors' help, conception still all comes from God. Why people question this is beyond me.

I believe that God creates people to become amazing like Him. So people that question medical interference should really never see a doctor, or take a Tylenol or even want to fix any ailment they get. God is good and, like any good soul, wouldn't He want to help us not suffer? Wouldn't He want to help us find ways to better ourselves?

If you cut your finger, it is helpful to put a Band-Aid over it to prevent further infection. Did God create the Band-Aid? Well He created the opportunity to invent that Band-Aid. How we use it is up to us. I am so thankful for Band-Aids, and so is my six-year-old. She often uses them as stickers, but she knows the real purpose. And that purpose is to help heal. That sounds like a God-given perk if you ask me.

I also believe that nothing is really created without God's approval. Doctors create amazing opportunities for our survival. I think God really only disapproves when we misuse what the intentional gift was for.

With all that said, since God intended us to honor and be like Him, we should want to continually make the world a better place. It says so in the Bible, which I have read and not just because I went to Catholic Schools.

I am very thankful for God's gifts. Thankful that He created medicinal usages for correcting bad eye sight, infertility and now labor pains. Speaking of that, "Where is that epidural technician? This is not working," I scream to myself.

I grimace again as I struggle to breathe. I extend my hands over my head in hopes of creating more room for my lungs to inhale. Instead, I think I just allowed the baby to stretch and now I have even less room.

"Where is that guy?" I beg my husband.

Wendy heads for the door and tells the nurse that I need more pain meds. She is a great advocate.

The nurse comes in and informs us that the epidural is running. She can even see when I last hit the button. I look at her and say, "I guess I am a wimp and I need more. The guy said he would be back in ten minutes. Maybe it's kinked again."

She reads the monitor's report and tells my husband that I shouldn't be feeling anything right now. Maybe I am imagining it. NOPE. This is one big one. I brace my foot against the cold steel and say a little prayer.

*"Dear Baby, I love you, but this is ridiculous. I know you want out and I want you out, but I can't do this unless you cooperate. Let me get a good breath in and maybe then I can get you out."*

I will miss the telepathy I have with her. Inhale, exhale, inhale, exhale—the nurse is counting breaths for me again. In walks my doctor.

"How you doing in here?"

The nurse explains that even with the epidural I am experiencing contractions.

He looks at the machine. "It's running," he says. Then he examines the last contraction report. "Good contractions. Let's see if you're ready to push. Do you feel like you want to push?" he asks me.

"I actually have to pee," I say.

"You can," he says.

I want to. I wish I could. I actually don't even care if I pee all over the floor and spray the entire room with a golden shower. I think if I pee, I will have less pressure.

I feel Doc's fingers. Actually, it might be his entire arm in me! He notices me flinch and retract within.

"Did you feel that?" he asks, obviously knowing the answer.

"Yes and now I really want to pee, but I can't."

"Can you try and push for me?" he asks. "Let's practice one during the next contraction."

Oh no, here I go. I can't push for nine hours. I'm so tired. Doc knows that I'm worried about having to push for too long. He knows what happened last time. He told me that if he was the doctor, he definitely would have given me a C-section. It was too risky to push for that long. Apparently, after your water breaks you really need to deliver within twenty-four hours or you risk infection. I was lucky that everything was fine.

My husband stands and grabs one of my legs; the nurse holds the other one. I push and hold my breath. The nurse is counting.

During my first delivery, I told the nurse to count to eight not ten because, as a former dance instructor, we count to eight. Either way, it doesn't help much. It really would help if I was a long-distance swimmer so I could hold my breath for five minutes at a clip.

When the push is over, Doc says, "I think we're ready to have a baby."

"What?" I exclaim as my husband verifies that I am ten centimeters and my daughter's three fairy godmothers sit on my right with excitement glowing in their eyes.

The next contraction is probably the longest and most dramatic one yet. I try to close my eyes as I clench every part of my body, but I can't. I'm watching Doc suit up and the nurses prepare for a landing. This is crazy. With my first delivery, the doctor didn't suit up until I had already pushed for eight hours, I've only pushed once and now he's dressing.

# 11

# *Naturally*

Doc has his white butcher's apron on, with blue rubber gloves and an interesting pair of goggles. Is he dressing to go scuba diving? I hope not. I don't even want my husband looking this close down there! Doc adjusts the spotlight at the foot of the bed to the center stage; my crotch.

Amidst all the chaos, my girlfriends ask if I want them to leave. I can't talk. Katie asks my husband if she can stay to take pictures. She is thinking about going back to school to be a labor and delivery nurse, so I suppose this will give her good experience. I mumble, "No crotch shots."

My husband is fumbling with the camcorder.
I told him to test it out, but he never did. I'm usually
the camera man, but I knew I couldn't video and give
birth at the same time, so I told him to figure it out.
He didn't and now I probably won't get a video of
her.

I cherish the video from my first daughter. I
love listening to her cooing and even crying in the
background. I had a girlfriend video her birth, but
only from the head up. I actually wish I could see
more, but my crotch is camera shy and it will be with
this baby, too. I hope he can figure it out. He doesn't
exactly have time to read the manual. But whatever
happens, happens. I have to go with the flow right
now. My heart is racing. This all seems to be
happening so fast.

The nurse asks Wendy if she will hold the
camcorder so my husband can hold my leg. I look at
Wendy and say, "No crotch shot."

The nurse is continually counting my breaths
and telling me when to bear down and push. Her
voice sounds so distant, but it's all I can concentrate
on.

I try to raise my hands over my head to get more room to breathe. Again, dumb move. Even the doctor asks why I'm doing that. I don't know. Obviously my body doesn't know what to do!

The pressure is intense. If my belly doesn't burst open soon, I will most definitely die. I can feel my veins protruding out through my eyeballs. Oh no, I hope I don't get black eyes. I've heard of some women blowing blood vessels while they push and getting black eyes. My lips are so dry. I want to ask for my chap stick but, at this point, there are no words that can form in my mouth or my brain.

"Good Push!" says the doctor. "Just a few more." He has a confused look on his face as he glances over my head at my husband. He shrugs his shoulders and says, "Nothing I can do now."

I want to ask what he's talking about, but I have to push. I want to push. I want to scream, but I can only imagine my exhale is pushing this baby OUT. I look at the nurse, she nods and asks, "Ready to go again?"

"Give me a minute." I say, but that doesn't happen, the wave comes and she commands the pushing with my breathing. She is OO OO OOing

113

like an owl. I am grunting and imagining blowing up a balloon. However, very quickly I'm out of air and need to inhale, but she is telling me not to yet. I look at my husband and he is just smiling.

"Again," the nurse says. I can't even see the Doctor's face anymore. Did he climb inside? I can't believe my husband is smiling about that. Again, I do as I had done the last time since she seemed to command that.

Wooooooooooooooooo....did I hear a pop?
I open my eyes and see the doctor holding my daughter. What the heck? How did that happen? I want to cry. I want to keep pushing. I can't believe I did it. I'm done! It's over? I think that was only four pushes or maybe five. Really? Really? Really?

She's out!

The fairy godmothers are watching from their prime seats, my husband is kissing me saying I did a good job and the doctor is putting her on my chest. She is beautiful, she is so tiny. I kiss her head and whisper, "Welcome" and "Thank you" at the same time.

The nurse is dabbing a towel on her and the doctor is handing my husband scissors. I wish I could watch that moment. Katie takes a photo. I know I will appreciate it. Separation. We are two people, I am just me and she is here. She is out. She is so beautiful.

My first daughter was just as beautiful. I try to compare them, but all I can think about is how excited my six-year-old will be to meet her. They are both from the same pod. Up until this moment, this baby has experienced everything my first one did, but she did it more quickly. More painful, but quicker.

The nurse takes her to the weighing station and my husband follows along with the camera crew. Doc is asking me for another push, so I am concentrating on pushing the placenta out. He forcefully pushes on my stomach, ugh…it works; it's out.

My husband yells, "She's over nine pounds!"

What? My head is dizzy. No wonder I was as big as a house! Our other daughter was six pounds.

"Hey Doc, that ultrasound today was wrong it measured her to be six or seven pounds! That's a big difference."

He smiles at me.

Wendy is coming over to congratulate me. The doctor grabs her arm and says, "Be careful the ground is wet there."

I assumed it was wet from some water source he used during delivery, but I found out later that my epidural WASN'T attached. It was leaking all over the floor! No wonder I had all those contractions and felt them!

Doc explained that he and my husband noticed it when I was pushing, but it was too late. That was the reason for the confused look on his face. Well, at least now they are over. I can't even be mad since now I'm holding my beautiful nine-pound daughter.

"What's her name?" Doc asks.

I look at my husband and he says, "We aren't sure yet."

I'm in disbelief. I did it; we did it. No, *I* did it! In a blink of an eye, she is here, in my arms. I really *was* pregnant; it wasn't a tumor. And I haven't died. Amazing.

All that pain, discomfort, and wondering what is going on with my body…it's over. I remember when I found out I was pregnant, I really didn't believe it. There was no Clomid involved and I'm certainly at the age when menopause could begin. When the doctor said I was pregnant I wasn't quite sure how it had happened.

Well, I know how and I think I actually know when it happened. But the surprise of naturally conceiving was and still is a shock. My husband and I had considered adoption, even going as far as taking all the classes and getting approval from the state that we would be competent parents. And then, two months before they wanted to do a home study, I chickened out and put it on hold.

My cold feet really had a lot to do with juggling building a house, running a business, and being mom to my six-year-old. I politely asked my husband if we could delay the process of adoption for a few months. I doubted if we needed to add to the chaos of our life. My heart broke for those children in foster care and, knowing my grandmother had been a foster mother to over forty babies in her life, inspired me. Little did I know that God was setting me up for a big surprise.

Now it's all over in a blink. It was just ten months ago that I went for a morning walk and felt odd. My belly had butterflies, my boobs were bouncing and sore, which was really odd since I am not well-endowed to say the least. They never bounce, except when I'm pregnant. I began to have an out of body experience, the trees seemed to be waving at me and I found myself questioning why I thought I was feeling so strange.

Mid stride I stopped and very hesitantly put my hand on my beautiful flat belly that I had worked so hard to get back over the last six years. This was going to be my first summer back in a bikini; I couldn't be pregnant.

"Is someone in there?" I asked, hoping to either get a kick for a response or just instantly know that I was thinking crazy. Nothing happened, but my first thought was to call a doctor. My heart began to race and I felt pressure to run home, get in my car, and go buy a test. The thought of that sounded crazy. A test?

Logically, I knew that I had to take a home test before I called the doctor with my premonition. My emotions were mixed. I walked at a snail's pace to delay the inevitable. I continued to talk to my belly and thought of how nuts it all sounded. I was probably going to set myself up for a disappointment, but which result was going to be disappointing? I had to take the test…at least for some relief.

I took the test and froze staring at the blue positive sign. It must be a mistake. Perhaps, a false positive. I questioned if I was hallucinating. Afraid to touch my own belly, I said out loud, "Really?!!?" A voice inside said, "Hi, Mom."

I knew then I was nuts. I needed to call the doctor, but which one—an OB or a psychiatrist?

My mind raced…my belly will grow, I'll gain weight, I'll be uncomfortable; I'll have to push a baby out again! I couldn't breathe with all the racing thoughts. I became nauseous at the thought of how I would tell my husband. He wouldn't believe it. He was probably going to think I had an affair.

Well, the doctor obviously confirmed that I was pregnant.

"Congratulations," the nurse said.

I just stared at her in silent shock. Inside an obnoxious voice was jumping for joy screaming, "Told you so, told you so, told you so!"

"Was this not planned?" the nurse asked.

"Uh, you guys told me I couldn't get pregnant and…well I'm just…are you sure?" I asked silently beaming in distress. "Could I just be in menopause?"

She laughed and gave me a prescription for prenatal vitamins.

That day wasn't the only day that I questioned if I was really pregnant. At almost every appointment, I would show up with a list of my ailments, and the doctor would just look and me and remind me I was pregnant. It seemed impossible.

During my first pregnancy I tracked every second. With this one, I often only concentrated on how surreal it was. Sometimes I felt like it was a dream. This pregnancy wasn't planned, so conceiving naturally wasn't what I was expecting. Then, again, maybe it was what I was expecting. I did wish for children long before I ever got married. I knew I wanted to be a mom. And I was. It seems selfish to create another child when there are so many who have this same wish and never get the opportunity.

I have to believe that God knows what He is doing. He creates many opportunities for life. And I have just given birth to one!

Amazing! I really was pregnant. Did I say that yet? Well I was. I wished for this child so many years before and I am just as awe struck now as I was with my first. It is the same, but different. I am complete. Our family is complete. I didn't even know something was missing in my life until this moment.

She is so peaceful. Angelic. Not squirming, and obviously comfortable to be in my arms and out of my little body. No wonder she didn't have any room in me, she weighs almost ten pounds. I hope I can make enough milk to sustain that figure! And hopefully once my feet stop swelling and my uterus contracts back to normal size, I will be back to my own size, too. Until then, I don't even care what I look like because I made her in me.

I am holding my daughter. Even without a name, I love her. She is perfect. She is heaven sent. She is beautiful. She will be amazing. I'm sure the perfect name will come, but right now I just want to hold her.

I kiss her and keep telling her I love her. I do. I love whoever she is and I'm glad she is in my arms and out of me!

*Dear Baby, Get Out!*

*Angela Grout*

# *A Note from the Author*

When my daughter turned six, we were looking at her baby photographs and she asked me to read part of her story. I looked at the mess of papers compiled to make her baby book and was inspired to ask her questions. I asked her what it was like to be in my belly and she said she wanted to get out.

"Why?" I asked.

"Mommy, it was too small and there wasn't enough to do."

Some people say children are nurtured, but from in the womb this child knew she needed to be busy and on the move. She has been busy since she was conceived, looking to do more all the time. She is not one to sit still very long and I know that she will make a difference in this world in some really big or really small way. She already has, in mine.

In case you're wondering what we named her. We named her Molly. Molly means, "wished for child." The perfect name came just as I knew it would. God has a perfect plan.

*Angela Grout*

*Dear Baby, Get Out!*

# *Acknowledgments*

I am humbled and extremely gracious to not only experience my pregnancies and motherhood, but also for the gift to write. God's love is amazing and I am appreciative for the opportunity to write stories that make me cherish God's gifts.

Thank you to my husband and my daughters for inspiring me to write and giving me an hour or two each day to tap on the keyboard. I used to hand write all my stories, journals and poems, but the ease of the computer allows me to move at a faster pace, but louder for them.

Life, kids, childbirth and writing can be complicated. There are often obstacles that we need encouragement, help and advice to journey through. Special thanks to Wendy Collins, Kay Coulter, Katie Dore, Kim Dottiwalla, Ava Grace, Betty Grout, Steven King, Steven Markley, Katie Lapolice, Joan Shuman, Emily Soloman, Shelley Sullivan, Mother Teresa, Dr. Fitzgerald, Dr. Howard Triesch and the staff at Baystate Medical Center. Thank you for helping me overcome some of my obstacles. You are inspirations to me.

Also thanks to my musically gifted cousin Sarah Lapolice for inspiring me through her music and words; "Something in You" and "11:11" have become songs of my soul. And thank you to Lisa Robie for my baby shower gift, the create your own baby storybook…which was the first seed to this story.

Special thanks to all the "moms" in my life that inspire motherhood, including and most importantly my own mom! (and Dad!)

For all the expectant moms reading this story, I wish you the perfect ending to your pregnancy. Relax, laugh and enjoy each moment for once your bundle gets here, you will have another journey! Have faith and remember each stage is only temporary, just as waiting to give birth is.

Life is a journey of stories to be told…one at a time. My hope is this story has helped you to move closer to your own story. Now, Get that Baby OUT!

*Angela Grout*

*Dear Baby, Get Out!*

■ ■ ■ ■ ■ ■ ■ ■ ■ ■ ■ ■ ■ ■ ■ ■ ■ ■ ■ ■ ■ ■ ■ ■ ■ ■ ■ ■ ■ ■ ■ ■ ■ ■ ■ ■ ■ ■ ■ ■ ■ ■ ■ ■

## ABOUT THE AUTHOR

Angela Grout lives in Massachusetts with her husband Gary and their greatest blessings, Maggie and Molly. She has a BA from Western New England University and has owned a flower shop for over twenty years.

Besides her passion for flowers and writing, Angela also enjoys reading, watersking, swimming, dancing, and watching her daughter's basketball games!

She has written several short stories and poems, sharing her faith and experinces. Many have been published in magazines and poetry journals. Her first book, An Angel's Journey was published in 2015.

*Dear Baby, Get Out!*

Made in the USA
Middletown, DE
02 June 2017